FR. MIKE S

ARE YOU SAVED?

THE CATHOLIC UNDERSTANDING
of SALVATION

ASCENSION
West Chester, Pennsylvania

Ascension
PO Box 1990
West Chester, PA 19380

1-800-376-0520
ascensionpress.com

Cover design: Rosemary Strohm

21 22 23 24 25 5 4 3 2 1

Printed in the United States of America
ISBN 978-1-950784-98-1

CONTENTS

Welcome to *The Curious Catholic*! Each booklet in this series is created to invite busy Catholics closer to God. Here Ascension offers you bite-sized discussions about important topics in day-to-day Catholic life. *The Curious Catholic* is designed to make it easy to fit spiritual growth into your day.

The booklets in this series are short and relatable with features that will help you apply what you read to your own life.*

Quotes and Bible verses throughout the booklets help you zero in on the key points.

Questions after each chapter prompt you to reflect and help you to dive deeper into the topic. We recommend praying or journaling with these questions as you make connections to your everyday life. The questions also make great prompts for small group discussion. Just keep in mind that not everyone in your group may feel comfortable answering the more personal questions.

Each chapter finishes with a challenge to act. These challenges invite you to enter into prayer, serve others, make a resolution for the week, and more.

We hope *The Curious Catholic* helps you along the way in your journey toward sainthood. May God bless you!

*Note: This booklet is adapted from a series of homilies given by Fr. Mike Schmitz.

Chapter 1

ARE YOU SAVED?

Have you ever been asked, "Are you saved?"

I was recently at the Newman Center's booth at the student activities fair here at the University of Minnesota Duluth, and a student came up who wanted to debate. He asked, "Are Catholics really Christians? Are you saved?"

In response to that question, "Are you saved?" people who have been raised Catholic can give many different responses. They might say, "I'm Catholic. Of course I'm saved." On the other hand, they might say, "Wait. What? Do we talk like that? Do we say those words?"

It's a good question. Do we say that as Catholics? The answer is yes. We do.

JESUS SAVES

Do we believe we are saved or are being saved? Yes is the answer, and it should not escape us. It should not be new. We just don't always talk like that. In fact, we don't always notice it. But as Catholics, we're all about the fact that we need to be saved.

Think about every single Sunday Mass. We say that Jesus came for our salvation when we pray, "For us men and for our salvation, he came down from heaven." At the point in the Mass called the mystery of faith, one of the options for the congregation's response is, "Save us, Savior of the world, for by your cross and resurrection, you have set us free." At every single Mass, we recognize that Jesus saves us.

The Bible talks about Jesus as the Savior constantly. When Gabriel appeared to Joseph, he said, "You shall call his name Jesus, for he will save his people from their sins" (Matthew 1:21). The name of Jesus means "God saves."

We believe that Jesus is the Savior, and we should be excited about it. But a lot of times when I talk to Catholics about the question, "Are you saved?" the answer is like, "Well, sure, I guess."

Saved from What?

Why are we not excited? Maybe we need to ask another question first. In fact, the question "Are you saved?" brings up another question: "Saved from what?" I think that's a legitimate question. We say that Jesus is the Savior, but what is he saving us from?

THE QUESTION "ARE YOU SAVED?" BRINGS UP ANOTHER QUESTION: "SAVED FROM WHAT?"

In his letter to Timothy, St. Paul says, "The saying is sure and worthy of full acceptance, that Christ Jesus came into the world to save sinners" (1 Timothy 1:15). When you hear that, you might think, "Oh, I get it—to save sinners. That means other people." But no—Jesus came to save sinners, and that means he came to save each of us.

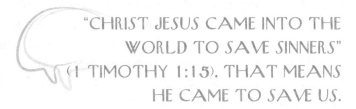

"CHRIST JESUS CAME INTO THE WORLD TO SAVE SINNERS" (1 TIMOTHY 1:15). THAT MEANS HE CAME TO SAVE US.

Jesus' name means "God saves." He is the Savior because he came to save us from our sins. And yet many of us might think, "That doesn't mean anything to me."

For a long time, it didn't mean anything to me. The *Catechism* says, "Since sin is universal, those who pretend not to need salvation are blind to themselves" (CCC 588). What does that mean? Since we all commit sins and we all experience the broken hearts that sins cause, we are not the people that we were actually made to be. That's just the truth of the matter. Since we all experience this, to pretend that we don't need salvation is to be blind.

I spent a big chunk of my life really blind. I was raised Catholic, so my parents made me go to Catholic school, and they made me go to Mass every single Sunday. The only reason I could get out of going to Mass is if I was too sick to do anything else for the rest of the day. So there were numerous times when I pretended to be sick. I would spend the day sitting on my bed rather than spending one hour in Mass. We didn't have any devices; we didn't have a computer; I couldn't even read books. I got to sit in my room by myself being so bored I wanted to throw up, but I thought that was a good trade because I didn't have to go to church. I didn't see the point of church.

Then, when I was fifteen or sixteen years old, something happened that changed my life. It was God's grace, but I don't know what sparked it. All of a sudden, I knew that sins were real in my life. I knew what the commandments were because I went to Mass and Catholic school. One day I just had this awareness of what sins were. I realized, "Wait, that's not just external. That's not just something other people do. That's me." I realized that sin was in my heart.

I was almost in panic as I realized, "That's what I do." And I was overwhelmed by the awareness that I can't forgive myself. I had a clear awareness that I needed a savior. It was like the moment in a cartoon when someone has a light bulb appear over their head. I realized that not only did I need a savior, but I had one. All of a sudden, everything that was ever told to me when I went to Mass made sense.

Up until then, I was a good kid. Up until then, when they brought me to confession, I was like, "I don't know. What did I do? I'm going to pull my sister's ponytail just to say something." But at that moment, I was given clarity about my broken heart. It was so clear to me that I need a savior and that for my whole life, I'd had a savior. I just hadn't cared.

I knew that Jesus, as my Savior, wanted to heal me in confession. So I just got on my bike and rode over to the priest's house. I knocked on his door at 10 o'clock on a Tuesday morning, and I went to confession, and it changed my life.

PAST, PRESENT, AND FUTURE

You might ask, "Father, that's when you were saved, right?" That day at age fifteen when I went to confession changed the rest of my life. That was part of my salvation, but salvation wasn't over for me in that moment.

The Catholic response to the question, "Are you saved?" is not necessarily the same as the non-Catholic response. This is the Catholic response: "I was saved at my baptism. I am currently being saved by God's grace. And I hope to be saved in the future."

I was saved at my baptism. I was saved when I went to confession when I was fifteen. I am being saved now. And I hope to be saved in the future. This is how we live as Catholics—we recognize that salvation is an event, but it's also a process. I was saved, I am being saved, and I hope to be saved.

> I WAS SAVED AT MY BAPTISM. I AM CURRENTLY BEING SAVED BY GOD'S GRACE. AND I HOPE TO BE SAVED IN THE FUTURE.

Think about the story of the Exodus. The people of God were slaves in Egypt, and God saved them. They didn't do anything to deserve it, yet he set them free. Then, when they journeyed into the wilderness, they needed him to keep saving them. Yes, they were saved when he set them free from slavery, but they still continued to need salvation. And they hoped that he would lead them to the Promised Land—that he would ultimately save them.

It is the same in our story.

TRANSFORMATION

We are broken by sin, so Jesus came to save us. Here's the reality of salvation: it's not just about past forgiveness, and it's not just about some future hope of heaven. Salvation is about a current transformation. You're being saved. God is doing something in your life. He's changing you right now.

This reality about God's offer of salvation is mind-blowing. Salvation is not just what people might call fire insurance, or a "get out of hell free" card. The Bible reveals that salvation is so much more. A Scripture scholar named Dr. Michael Barber wrote a book on salvation called *Salvation: What Every Catholic Should Know* that will give us a lot of insight in the pages ahead and be a thread that runs through this booklet. Barber said that salvation is being saved from being un-Christ-like.[1] That hit me really hard.

SALVATION IS BEING SAVED FROM BEING UN-CHRIST-LIKE.

Salvation transforms your life and my life to be like Christ. What does that mean? It means you have a Father. It means you have hope. It means you have life, and it means you are loved.

God is changing you right now, and you participate. You're actually cooperating with salvation. It's about a way of living in response to God's love.

REFLECT

Have you ever been asked the question, "Are you saved?"
How did you respond?

Why do you think it's important for Catholics to talk
about salvation?

Are there moments in your life when you recognize your
own sin? In those moments, do you respond by asking for
God's grace, or with despair?

What does it mean to you that Jesus is your Savior?
Is Jesus a part of your life because you need him and
appreciate him, or is he just nice to have around if and
when you feel like connecting with him?

What have your experiences with confession been
like? Do you have any fear, worry, or doubt about the
sacrament?

What does it mean to you that salvation isn't just an
event, but it's also a process? What does this process look
like in your life?

Are there any *areas of your life that are un-Christ-like right now?*

Salvation is not *just about past forgiveness or a future hope of heaven. Have you ever thought of salvation as also being a part of your present, day-to-day life? Can you see it in your own life? In what ways?*

ACT

In prayer*, ask Jesus to show you what he came to save you from and what he made you for. If you haven't been to confession lately, find your parish's times or book an appointment to go this week!*

Chapter 2

SAVED FROM FATHERLESSNESS

"Are you saved?" Often, we don't think about this question because we don't really feel the need to be saved. In fact, we often ask, "Well, what do I need to be saved from?" We need to be saved from our sins, but what does that mean?

In the first chapter, we talked about Dr. Michael Barber's book, and we said that salvation means you are being saved from being un-Christ-like. When your salvation began, you were brought into the relationship that the Son has with his Father. You were saved from an orphan spirit and from being abandoned.

Think about this. When you're baptized, you're brought into the relationship that the Son has with his Father. The love the Father has for the Son actually begins to live inside of you. That's the Holy Spirit. If you are in a state of grace right now, the love the Father has for the Son lives inside of you right now.

This is really churchy, abstract language, so we'll break it down. So many of us are walking through this world as if we had been abandoned, as if we don't have a Father. Yet one of the first things and the ultimate things that Jesus saves us from is fatherlessness. That's the first thing it means to be saved from being un-Christ-like.

JESUS SAVES US FROM FATHERLESSNESS.

You might think of salvation with different images, and the Council of Trent—a major Catholic council in the 1500s—used some of them. An image of salvation is that you transfer from darkness to light. You transfer from the kingdom of slavery to freedom and forgiveness and righteousness. Amid these images, the number one image from the Council of Trent is the image of being transferred from being a slave to being a son, being actually adopted by our Father. Because we're saved, we can say to God, "You're our Father now."

THE PRODIGAL SON

But here's our problem. Here's the mess. So many of us have been adopted—we've been saved—but we don't want to live in the Father's house. He's made us into his children, but we're like the prodigal son. Remember how the prodigal son walked away from his father?

THE PRODIGAL SON

"There was a man who had two sons; and the younger of them said to his father, 'Father, give me the share of property that falls to me.' And he divided his living between them. Not many days later, the younger son gathered all he had and took his journey into a far country, and there he squandered his property in loose living ... [Then] he arose and came to his father. But while he was yet at a distance, his father saw him and had compassion, and ran and embraced him and kissed him" (Luke 15:11-13, 20).

Maybe you go to Mass every week but you want to be somewhere else. Like the prodigal son, you're thinking, "Yeah, yeah, God is my Father, and he loves me and whatever. But I don't like this whole church thing, and I still haven't made up my mind whether I'm going to live in his house." Maybe you're thinking you might put faith on hold for the next few years and not actually live as a son or a daughter of God. Some of us have that temptation in our hearts to try to live life on our own.

Or maybe we're committed to Sunday Mass, but we still don't want to live like God is our Father. Maybe that's even worse, because we say to God, "OK, here's the deal. I'll show up to Mass. Maybe I'll even come to a Bible study once in a while. But praying every day? That's not an option. I'll give you Sunday and, sure, I'll work for you occasionally, but I don't want anything more." We think our arrangement is that we will stay in God's house, but we are going to live there like a slave. It's as if we're saying to him, "I don't want to live here as your daughter or your son."

THE SPIRIT OF ADOPTION

But you've been adopted. You've been saved. Why live like you don't have a Father? Why do that when our Father has claimed us?

St. Paul said, "You received a spirit of adoption, through which we cry, 'Abba, Father!'" (Romans 8:15, NAB). When St. Paul said this, he was probably thinking of the Roman laws about adoption. According to ancient Roman law, if you were adopted, it meant at least four things.

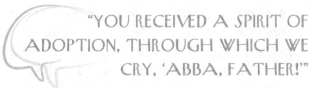

"YOU RECEIVED A SPIRIT OF
ADOPTION, THROUGH WHICH WE
CRY, 'ABBA, FATHER!'"

(Romans 8:15, NAB).

The first thing it meant is that you were given a new identity. You were given a new name and new relationships, so you were no longer the person you were. Second, it meant that any debts you owed were canceled. Third, adoption meant that you had the full rights and all the inheritance of any natural-born child. You weren't valued less because you were adopted.

The fourth thing adoption meant in ancient Rome absolutely blew my mind when I heard it. Under Roman law, parents could actually abandon their natural-born child. If the parents found their baby to be defective—maybe not the sex they wanted— they could just leave the baby at the dump to be exposed to the elements or eaten by dogs. If their child had some kind of birth defect, they could abandon their baby. But under Roman law, parents could not abandon a person they adopted.

If parents found out that their adopted son or daughter had some defect or there was something amiss, they were prohibited by Roman law from walking away from their adopted child. If you were adopted, you could never be abandoned.

You've been saved by a God who does not do what a Roman father could do to his natural-born child. You've been saved by a God who looks at your defects and does not abandon you. When St. Paul says that you have been adopted, he is saying that you have been saved by a God who will never abandon you.

THE FATHER'S LOVE

God knows you're broken. He knows you're not perfect. But he says, "That's my daughter. Now she's mine, and I'll never walk away from her. This is my son. He's mine, and I will never abandon him."

As human parents, we can do wrong and walk away and abandon our children. I know some people reading this have been abandoned by their parents and by the people they relied on. As human beings, we can walk away from God, too. But God never abandons his children. In this life, we can walk away from him, but God never walks away from us. The Father does not force us to love him. He does not force us to accept the gift of his very own divine and eternal life that he offers us, but he is waiting to save us if we return to him.

Jesus came to save us from being un-Christ-like. That means you are absolutely, definitively saved from fatherlessness if you choose to live in the Father's house. When the Father says, "This is my child," one of the many things he's saying is, "I will never let go. I will never abandon you. I will never walk away."

Are you saved? Am I saved? Yes, God saved me when he made me his child. He is saving me so I can live and love as his child. And he will continue to save me, so I can hope that one day I will be able to walk into the Father's house to live there forever as his child.

REFLECT

Have you ever felt like God would reject you for your defects or failures? How do we know he won't? Did understanding what adoption is help you realize this?

Does knowing that you have a Father in heaven who loves you change the way you think about yourself?

Are there any areas of your life where you think God wants to bring you from darkness into light?

Is it hard to believe that God will not abandon you?

Have you walked away from God before in any situations in your life? How can you act differently in the future to stay with God instead?

What does it mean that you're a child of God?

To be saved from being un-Christ-like is to be saved from fatherlessness. Is it difficult to let God love you as a good father would love you?

ACT

Having God as our Father *changes everything. Identify a change that you can make in your life to live as a child of God, and make that change!*

Chapter 3

SAVED FROM HOPELESSNESS

Have you thought about the national debt lately? As of June 2021, the United States' national debt is $28.2 trillion.[2] Can you imagine $28.2 trillion? It's one of those things where we're like, "I'm glad I don't have to figure that out." It's so huge, we might think there's no way it's ever going to get paid, but it's so far away from us that it's not a part of our daily lives. If we want to, we can just not think about it, and it probably won't affect us anytime soon.

But did you know that the average college student loan debt is $39,000?[3] That's a little more personal. The average family household debt in America is $145,000.[4] That's what the average family owes, including mortgage, auto loans, credit card debt, school debt, and so forth.

The national debt is one of the things I don't necessarily have to think about. As long as it's far away from me, I can be kind of indifferent. But when it comes to my own personal debt, it can be really easy to get discouraged. In fact, it can be really easy to feel hopeless.

HOPELESSNESS

For a lot of us, our debt is more than we can pay unless a rich uncle comes out of nowhere and says, "Oh, here's a few hundred thousand dollars." I owe such a large debt; I cannot pay it back. It is so easy to feel stuck and hopeless in the face of knowing that I actually don't have a way to pay back what I owe.

We've been talking about the question, "Are you saved?" As Catholics, we don't always talk in these terms, although we pray about being saved, and we know that Scripture says that the Son of Man came to seek and to save what was lost. But a lot of times we have a question: "OK, I need to be saved from what?" We don't feel the need to be saved. We're kind of like, "I'm doing fine."

In the last chapter, we talked about the reality that so many of us are walking through this world like orphans. So many of us are walking through this world without God, who is our Father. And so we recognized that one of the first things and the ultimate things that Jesus saves us from is fatherlessness.

Jesus also saves us from hopelessness. He has to because we are in debt, and we can't save ourselves.

JESUS SAVES US FROM HOPELESSNESS.

A DEBT I CAN'T PAY

Remember that Gabriel the angel appeared to Joseph and said, "You'll name him Jesus"—specifically because Jesus would save his people from their sins? This is the reality for every one of us: We all need to be saved from our sins. In the Bible, sin equals debt. Since I have sin, it's like I owe something now. The problem is that this sin is a debt I can't pay. I owe something more than I can pay back.

THIS IS THE REALITY FOR EVERY ONE OF US: WE ALL NEED TO BE SAVED FROM OUR SINS.

We might go for years without really recognizing that we have sin in our hearts and that we owe a debt we can't pay. I talked about how that was true for me—I went to Mass and knew the commandments because I went to Catholic school, but it didn't mean anything to me. When I was fifteen or sixteen, I suddenly realized, "Wait, that is sin that I have in my own heart." I suddenly recognized what I owed. I went from being indifferent to the sin to knowing that I owed a debt that I couldn't pay.

If you've never gotten to that point, this might be a little boring. But if you have looked into your heart, you know that sense of owing something you can't pay. You have recognized, "OK, I actually do have this sin. I have something that I owe that I have absolutely no way of paying back." And a debt brings us a sense of hopelessness because it is something we can't deal with.

ENSLAVED

Now, of course, debts are nothing new. In fact, the Bible talks a lot about debts.

In biblical times, if you were Jewish and got yourself into debt, you were responsible for paying off what you owed. The book of Leviticus talks about this very clearly. But here's the problem. If you couldn't pay off your debt, you'd have to sell your stuff. And there was no time to waste; you had to do it as soon as you could.

In fact, sometimes your debt was so huge that you had to sell your ancestral home. Now for us, losing our house would feel terrible, but for the Israelites, it was a thousand times worse. When the Jews were brought to the Promised Land, God gave them this land. So a house for an Israelite family in biblical times was not just a house. It was the land that belonged to their father and grandfather, all the way back to when Joshua led the people of Israel across the Jordan River into the Promised Land. And if you were in debt, you would have to sell that home. You were erasing your family's history.

But there were times when that still wasn't enough. When you couldn't pay off your debt by selling your stuff or even your home, you had the opportunity to sell yourself into slavery. Sometimes, you'd actually sell your spouse and your children as well as yourself into slavery. The Jews saw that as an evil, but they thought it was a necessary evil. Why? Because someone lent you the money, and you needed to give it back to the person who lent it to you. Slavery was not perfect, but it was almost their only option. There was only one other way to pay the debt.

REDEEMED

If you couldn't pay your debt, the one way to save yourself and everyone you loved from slavery was family. Family was your one hope.

In ancient Israel, family was important. If you entered a covenant with someone, you became family. So if you married someone, you and your spouse became part of each other's families. If tribes came together and made a covenant with each other, then they would actually be family. A Jewish scholar at Harvard named Jon Levenson who talked about this said the primary duty of family was to love each other. Love was not just warm feelings—love meant that family members had a solemn duty to remain unwaveringly faithful and committed. In practical terms, if you were indebted so much that you were hopeless, a family member could be your redeemer.

A family member could buy you back, but it had to be a family member. In the Bible, this is called the kinsman-redeemer. Your brother or uncle or cousin or someone else in your family could ransom you to save you from slavery and pay a debt that you could not pay. In the depths of your hopelessness, your family member could step in and give you your life back.

In St. Paul's letter to Timothy, he says that Jesus gave his life as a ransom for all (see 1 Timothy 2:6). What he's saying is that Jesus is our kinsman-redeemer. We owe a debt that we cannot pay. We find ourselves stuck in hopelessness. And Jesus gave himself as a ransom.

"CHRIST JESUS ... GAVE HIMSELF AS
A RANSOM FOR ALL"

(1 Timothy 2:6).

Think about the Incarnation. "Incarnation" is a fancy word for God becoming one of us. The whole reason why God became a human being is so that you and I could be his brothers and sisters. Why? So he could redeem us.

That's the whole reason. Why did Jesus come to earth? Why did God become one of us? So he could be our brother to redeem us. Only a family member could ransom someone from debt; only a family member could buy that person back. And so, as the letter to the Hebrews says, God became like us, a brother in all things, to redeem us (see Hebrews 2:17).

> JESUS CAME TO EARTH SO HE COULD BE
> OUR BROTHER TO REDEEM US.

That means Jesus "took what was ours to be his very own so that we might have all that was his."[5] An ancient saint, St. Cyril of Alexandria, said this. Jesus took to himself our humanity so he could give us his divinity. Jesus took to himself our weakness so he could give us his strength. Jesus took to himself our brokenness and lowliness so he could give us his wholeness and make us like himself. He took our debt so he could give us his mercy.

> JESUS "TOOK WHAT WAS OURS TO BE
> HIS VERY OWN SO THAT WE MIGHT
> HAVE ALL THAT WAS HIS."

Remember, the heart of salvation is being saved from being un-Christ-like. Salvation is being saved not just from owing a debt but from walking through this world and not looking like God or living like God or loving like God.

IT ISN'T FAIR

At this point some people are probably thinking, "Wait, let's go back to the beginning. This isn't fair. I didn't break the world. It was already broken. I didn't bring sin into the world. I didn't eat the apple." In fact, I know a lot of people who say things like, "I didn't choose to be born in a broken world. I didn't choose to be born into debt." And I get that. You're right. Evil isn't fair. Suffering and death aren't fair. That's true.

But here's something else that's true. God knows this. He understands our struggle better than anyone because he "has been tempted as we are, yet without sinning" (Hebrews 4:15). This is very important. Christ Jesus came into this world "not to condemn the world, but that the world might be saved through him" (John 3:17). St. Paul says that God "desires all men to be saved and to come to the knowledge of the truth. For there is one God, and there is also one mediator between God and man, the man Jesus Christ, who gave himself as a ransom for all" (1 Timothy 2:4-6).

It isn't fair that you and I wake up every morning with all these pains in our hearts, but it also wasn't fair that God was completely innocent and took upon himself for every single one of us our brokenness, our pains, our sufferings, our temptations. He took all of those into his own heart on purpose.

It's not fair that it's broken, but it's also not fair that you've been made whole. Salvation is a gift. It's undeserved. It's unmerited. It's unearned. It's just given. Actually, that's what the word "grace" means.

When St. Paul uses that word in the New Testament, it's not a theological term. "Grace" just means "present" or "gift." No one ever deserves a gift or works for a gift. We just receive the gift. The truth of the matter is, we're saved by a gift. It's grace.

WORKING IN LOVE

People who ask, "Are you saved?" often misunderstand what we believe as Catholics. Many times, they think that Catholics believe we work for our salvation. That's not actually the case. Here's what we believe about how salvation works: we believe that we are saved by grace through faith working itself out in love.

> ## WE ARE SAVED BY GRACE THROUGH FAITH WORKING ITSELF OUT IN LOVE.

Let's think about this. We are saved by grace, the complete gift of God. It's unmerited, unearned, undeserved. We are saved by grace through faith. Faith is our response to grace, which is just a yes to God. It's an obedience to God working itself out in love. That's the core, the whole heart of everything. It comes down to love.

This idea that love is at the heart of everything sounds sappy, but it's not. Because what do you see at the front of every Catholic church? It's the crucifix.

Some Christians believe that when you look at the crucifix, what you're seeing is the Father pouring out his anger and wrath and judgment upon Jesus. But that is not what we believe. Because the heart of the crucifix is love.

> ## THE HEART OF THE CRUCIFIX IS LOVE.

Here's the deal. Jesus' love is infinite. When we look at the crucifix, we can see that this is about how much he loved. The crucifix is not about the Father pouring out his wrath on Jesus. The crucifix shows the Son pouring out his infinite love to the Father.

WHAT COMES NEXT

We are saved by grace through faith working itself out in love. The ransom, the payment of the debt, is just the beginning.

The point is not just to have your debt cleared. The whole point is what comes after that.

If you're in debt and someone said, "Hey, you should start investing," you'd be like, "I can't invest. I've got this debt." If someone said, "What you should really think about is planning that dream vacation," you'd be like, "Listen, buddy, I don't have any money. I'm just stuck." When you're stuck in that hopelessness of debt, you can't think about anything after that. But what if someone paid your debt? What would you do next?

I think about St. Maximilian Kolbe.[6] He was a Polish man and a Franciscan. During World War II, he was taken into the concentration camp in Auschwitz because he was a priest. Auschwitz had a whole section where they tortured and abused priests. When you hear about Maximilian Kolbe's story, often all you think about is the end of his life in Auschwitz. But if you had lived in that era, you would have known that Maximilian Kolbe founded a number of magazines. He created opportunities to reach out and evangelize people. He was a missionary to Japan. He was an influential person who led thousands of people throughout Europe.

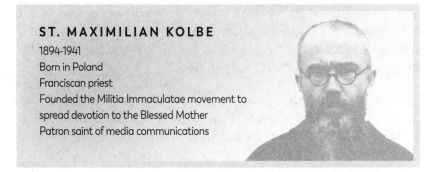

ST. MAXIMILIAN KOLBE
1894-1941
Born in Poland
Franciscan priest
Founded the Militia Immaculatae movement to
spread devotion to the Blessed Mother
Patron saint of media communications

Then Maximilian Kolbe was sent to the prison camp, and one night a man escaped from Auschwitz. So the next day the guards rounded up all the prisoners and said they were going to randomly select ten people to die because this man escaped. The name of the tenth person selected to die was Francis. He was another Polish man. When they called him forward, he fell to his knees and begged for mercy. He said, "Please do not kill me. I have a wife and children. Please let me live." Then Maximilian Kolbe stepped forward. Remember, Maximilian was very influential, and he could have decided that people needed him to live, but he said, "Please let me die for this man."

The guard said, "Why would you want to do that?" Maximilian Kolbe's answer was very simple. He said, "Because I'm a Catholic priest." Just think about the risk that he took. He was in a concentration camp where the guards could have just thrown that sacrifice away and killed both Francis and Maximilian. But instead they said, "OK, Francis. You go back to the group. Maximilian, you go into the starvation bunker."

Maximilian stayed in the bunker for two weeks without food and finally died from a lethal injection. But Francis lived. At that moment, when he was called forward to be the tenth person to die, Francis was hopeless. Because of Maximilian's sacrifice, Francis was freed. But the point wasn't just to be free from death; the point was to live.

Francis went on to live for over fifty years. And his friends and family said that as long as Francis had breath in his lungs, he believed it was his duty to tell as many people as possible about what Fr. Maximilian did for him. See, the story doesn't end when the debt gets paid. The story just starts when the debt gets paid.

LIVING

We're like Francis. We've been freed from death. Our debt has been paid off. I was hopeless because I owed a debt I could not pay, but now I am free because Jesus paid that debt he did not owe.

So what comes next? What are you going to do now that your debt has been paid and you're free from that weight on your shoulders?

> WHAT ARE YOU GOING TO DO
> WITH YOUR LIFE NOW THAT YOUR
> DEBT HAS BEEN PAID?

Now that you're free, you have power and grace—the gift of God—inside you. What's next? He poured himself out. Where are you going to pour yourself out? Where are you going to give your heart like he gave his heart?

You can have the opportunity to move from hopelessness to living a debt-free life. What is the first thing you're going to do with that freedom?

REFLECT

Have you been in debt before? What did that feel like?

What does freedom from debt look like? How should we respond to the salvation Christ has won for us?

What struck you from the story of St. Maximilian Kolbe? How is God calling you further into sacrificial love, like St. Maximilian? How is he calling you to respond to his sacrificial love, like Francis?

What has God saved you from? Give thanks!

Can you think of a recent experience (past or present) when you have felt so hopeless that you believed no good could come from it?

Jesus paid a debt he didn't owe so that we could be saved. When you look at it from that perspective, does it change your attitude to gratitude?

The crucifix shows Christ's love for us in a special way. When you look at a crucifix, what can you learn about his love for you?

The payment of the debt is not the end of the story. The payment of the debt is just the beginning of the story. So what is the next step for you?

ACT

Spend some time in front of a crucifix and think about the freedom that Christ has won for you. What are you going to do with this freedom?

Chapter 4

SAVED FROM LIFELESSNESS

I'm not sure how many people today are collectors, but collecting used to be really popular. I'm sure you know people who have collected baseball cards or bottle caps or comic books. My older sisters, when they were little, collected spoons. It wasn't even their choice—my parents and my grandparents would come back from a trip and be like, "Here's a spoon. Don't use it. Keep it in the packaging."

That's how collecting works, isn't it? If you're a collector of something, like Star Wars memorabilia, you keep those things in the packaging. The reason you're collecting them is not to use them but just so you can have them. Collectors can spend a lot of time, energy, and money just to have "the thing"—the rookie card, or the comic book, or whatever it is.

I think collecting memorabilia is a fine hobby. There's no problem with that. But there can be a problem if we live our lives like collectors. For some of us, our lives become just like collecting stuff, and we don't necessarily realize it.

A lot of times, the reason we show up to anything is to get something. We go to college to get a degree; we go to work to get a paycheck. Our lives can be this way. We can have the attitude, "I'm here to get." We might say, "I'm not going to go to that class because I don't get anything out of it." Or "I'm not going to go to that small group at church because I don't really get anything out of it." Our lives can ultimately become a pattern of thinking, "If I'm not going to get anything, I'm not going to be there."

I read an article by an antique dealer who said that people don't collect things like they used to. He said that one reason is that they collect experiences. Instead of filling a garage with stuff, people have many photos and a lot of experiences.

That's one of the reasons I think we experience the fear of missing out. We might spend a lot of time with friends, and at one level we might do that because we want to connect with them. But on another level, we might spend time with them because we're afraid that we won't have the experience if we say no. And so we can end up becoming collectors, living life to get experiences. That is exhausting.

"QUIET DESPERATION"

In his famous book *Walden*, Henry David Thoreau wrote these words: "The mass of men lead lives of quiet desperation." He said the reason he moved to a cabin on Walden Pond was to break free of this race to collect stuff.[7] People feel like they need to acquire stuff. Even people who have a lot try to collect more. But if we spend our lives collecting, will we look back at the end of our lives and say it was worth it?

In the book of the prophet Amos, Amos describes people who are living large. They're collecting experiences; they're collecting joys and pleasures. Amos says that they "lie upon beds of ivory" (Amos 6:4). Let that sink in. How many elephants have to die to make a bed of ivory? Amos continues, saying they "drink wine in bowls" (Amos 6:6). Have you ever seen those glasses that you can almost fit a whole bottle of wine into? The people Amos describes have collected a lot, but they still find themselves lifeless at the end of the day.

The parable of the rich man is a perfect example (see Luke 16:19-31). The way Jesus describes him, you can tell he had collected a lot of stuff. He dressed in fine linen and purple garments. That means the most expensive cloth he could wear. He dined sumptuously each day, not just a few times a year. And at the end of his life, he realized his life was empty. He could look at himself and say, "What was my life worth?"

SAVED FROM LIFELESSNESS

This is the reality for every single one of us. When I find myself showing up just to "get," what happens at the end of the story? At the end of my life, I can realize, "I just showed up to get, and I ended up living a lifeless life. All the things I collected, I just kept in the package."

We've been talking about salvation. Although we know that Jesus is our Savior, we often wonder, "What is he saving me from?" First, we talked about the fact that Jesus saves us from being orphans. He saves us from fatherlessness because God makes us his sons and daughters. Second, we talked about how we all owe a debt that we cannot pay, so Jesus paid a debt he did not owe. He saves us from the hopelessness that almost always comes along with indebtedness.

And now, third, we're going to talk about the fact that God saves us from lifelessness. If I show up just to get, it's like I spend my life collecting things and keep them in the package. And there's a danger that I can do this with God's grace.

GOD SAVES US FROM LIFELESSNESS.

I can think that being saved means just showing up to get grace. I can find myself being the passive recipient of God's grace and thinking that's fine. If I do that, I collected it, but I'm still lifeless.

Every person who has been baptized has been given the Holy Spirit, and yet sometimes we look around in church, and we're like, "Are you sure? Do we have the Holy Spirit?" Or we look in the mirror. Could someone ask, "Are you sure? Do you have the Holy Spirit?" If I'm just being the passive recipient of grace, I'm not being changed.

ALIVE IN CHRIST

Remember what Dr. Michael Barber said about salvation? He said salvation is being saved from being un-Christ-like, from not being like Jesus.

Think about Jesus and his life on this earth. No one was more present than Jesus, no one was more powerful, and no one loved people better. Honestly, in the history of the world, there was no one more alive than Jesus.

If you read the Gospels, you can see that Jesus doesn't show up to collect. He doesn't say, "If I get off this boat among all these lepers and people who need healing, what am I going to get from this?" Whenever he showed up anywhere, Jesus was always saying, "Where can I give? What can I do?" He's the source of all grace. He gives us the Holy Spirit—for the Holy Spirit proceeds from the Father and the Son. All that life comes from him. And salvation is being saved from living in a way that is unlike him. It's being saved from lifelessness.

Good Works

Think of what Jesus' life looked like. We read in Acts, "He went about doing good" (Acts 10:38). He did good works. Sometimes the idea of "good works" brings up the classic Catholic versus Protestant dilemma. Are we saved through faith or through works? We are saved by grace through faith working itself out in love.

> ## SALVATION
> We are saved by grace through faith working itself out in love.
> Ephesians 2:8-9: "You have been saved through faith; and this is not your own doing, it is the gift of God—not because of works, lest any man should boast."
> James 2:14, 17: "What does it profit, my brethren, if a man says he has faith but has not works? ... Faith by itself, if it has no works, is dead."

Ephesians chapter 2 points out that faith is really important. We read, "For by grace you have been saved through faith" (Ephesians 2:8). Remember, grace means gift. Salvation has been a free gift, unmerited, unearned, undeserved. St. Paul says, "You have been saved through faith; and this is not your own doing, it is the gift of God—not because of works, lest any man should boast" (Ephesians 2:8-9).

At the same time, we have to ask the question: If I'm saved from lifelessness—if I'm called to be like Jesus—doesn't that mean I have to act? Absolutely yes. This is an important question because one of Martin Luther's rallying cries in the Protestant Reformation was *sola fide*, or "faith alone."

It's really interesting to ask what the Bible teaches about being saved by faith alone. Where does the Bible have the words "faith alone"? In the entire Bible, the only place where those two words are next to each other is in the letter of James. It's when James says, "You see that a man is justified by works and not by faith alone" (James 2:24).

What else does James have to say? James is super sassy. I like the sassy saints. James talks about this whole question of how we are saved. Are we saved just by believing? No, James says, "What does it profit, my brethren, if a man says he has faith but has not works? Can his faith save him?" (James 2:14). James talks about faith and works.

It's like James is getting warmed up. He goes on to give an example: "If a brother or sister is poorly clothed and in lack of daily food, and one of you says to them, 'Go in peace, be warmed and filled,' without giving them the things needed for the body, what does it profit?" (James 2:15-16). We've all had that experience. We've seen other people in distress and felt bad for them, and we've thought, "I'm a good person because I felt bad." James is like, "No, you're not. Do something to help." St. James says, "Faith by itself, if it has no works, is dead" (James 2:17).

He continues, "But some one will say, 'You have faith and I have works.' Show me your faith apart from your works, and I by my works will show you my faith" (James 2:18). And this is where he gets super sassy. He says, "You believe God is one; you do well. Even the demons believe—and shudder" (James 2:19). James is telling us that faith without works is lifeless.

Faith without works is lifeless, and Jesus came to save us from lifelessness. He came to save us from being collectors who just hold on to things and don't use them. God wants us to do more than merely collect grace; he wants us to become active participants in his work and his mercy.

FAITH WITHOUT WORKS IS LIFELESS, AND JESUS CAME TO SAVE US FROM LIFELESSNESS.

MERCY

Matthew chapter 25 helps us recognize that we're judged on the basis of our works. This is the story of the last judgment—the King comes at the end of time and separates everyone, the sheep from the goats. To those on his right, he says, "Come into the dwelling of my heavenly Father, because I was hungry and you gave me food. I was thirsty and you gave me drink, and I was in need and you helped me." And they say, "Lord, when did we see you hungry and thirsty and in need?" And he says, "As often as you did it for the least of my brethren, you did it for me. So come into heaven." And to the others he says, "Depart from me. You are cursed, because I was hungry and you didn't feed me. I was naked and you didn't clothe me." They say, "Lord, when did we see you like that and not serve your needs?" And he says, "Every time you didn't do it to one of the least of my brethren" (see Matthew 25:31-46).

THE LAST JUDGMENT

"Then the King will say to those at his right hand, 'Come, O Blessed of my Father, inherit the kingdom prepared for you from the foundation of the world; for I was hungry and you gave me food, I was thirsty and you gave me drink, I was a stranger and you welcomed me, I was naked and you clothed me, I was sick and you visited me, I was in prison and you came to me ... Truly I say to you, as you did it to one of the least of these my brethren, you did it to me'" (Matthew 25:34-36, 40).

At the end of time, we're all judged based on our works—what we do. We are judged based on whether we were lifeless or full of life, whether we were simply passive recipients of grace or active participants in God's work to transform the world.

God doesn't just want us to receive his mercy; he wants us to be agents of his mercy. He doesn't just want us to receive his redemption and salvation; he wants us to be agents of salvation and redemption.

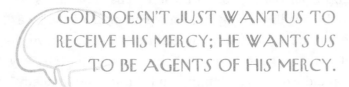

GOD DOESN'T JUST WANT US TO RECEIVE HIS MERCY; HE WANTS US TO BE AGENTS OF HIS MERCY.

My proof for saying that is in the Bible. St. Paul writes to Timothy, "You, man of God … aim at righteousness, godliness, faith, love, steadfastness, gentleness. Fight the good fight of the faith; take hold of the eternal life" (1 Timothy 6:11-12). Be active. Come fully alive.

You know the little action figures in packages that people collect, like Boba Fett and Luke Skywalker? Don't be like an action figure that's still in the box. God has been giving you his grace your entire life in order to save you from lifelessness—so use it.

ACTION

You may be thinking, "I don't have anything to offer. I'm not a superhero. What do you mean, Jesus saves me from lifelessness? What can I do?"

In his Letter to the Colossians, St. Paul tells us how powerful grace is. He says that God can use everything. In Colossians 1:24,

St. Paul writes, "Now I rejoice in my sufferings for your sake, and in my flesh I am completing what is lacking in the sufferings of Jesus for the sake of his body, the church."

"NOW I REJOICE IN MY SUFFERINGS FOR YOUR SAKE"
(Colossians 1:24).

Let's break this down because it's a big statement. St. Paul is saying that he rejoices in his sufferings. So being full of life doesn't mean being free from pain. Then he says that he's making up for what is lacking in the sufferings of Jesus. What does that mean? What was lacking in Christ's life, death, and resurrection that St. Paul needs to make up for?

St. John Paul II answered that question. He said that nothing is lacking in the sufferings of Christ, but God gives us a chance to participate in his work of redemption.[8] So that you and I could come alive and be saved from lifelessness, God extends to us a particle of his cross. If we embrace it and use it, it can actually transform the world. God doesn't need our help, but he wants us to join in with him.

GOD EXTENDS TO US A PARTICLE OF HIS CROSS. IF WE EMBRACE IT, IT CAN ACTUALLY TRANSFORM THE WORLD.

God is a very powerful Father. He can save the world on his own. But he's like a dad who gives his kids a chance to help him build something. A dad doesn't need a kid's help. But this is the amazing mystery of God's love for you. He doesn't just want you to sit down and watch him.

GOD IS AT WORK IN YOU

St. Paul's letter to the Ephesians doesn't stop where we stopped. Remember, it says, "For by grace you have been saved through faith; and this is not your own doing, it is the gift of God—not because of works, lest any man should boast" (Ephesians 2:8-9). Then it goes on. Verse 10 says, "For we are his workmanship, created in Christ Jesus for good works, which God prepared beforehand, that we should walk in them."

In Philippians 2:12, St. Paul writes, "Work out your own salvation with fear and trembling." He calls us to work, to engage, and to embrace this act of participation, for God is at work in us both to will and to work for his good pleasure. So yes, by grace we've been saved—it is a complete gift. But St. Paul is also saying that God is at work in us every time we do something good. When he extends that particular cross to you and you embrace it and rejoice in your sufferings for the salvation of the world, that's actually his grace to you.

We are doing good works, but we don't do them on our own. Imagine this scene. Did you ever see a two-year-old and his dad playing basketball? The dad puts the basketball in the two-year-old's hands, and then he lifts the toddler up to the hoop and says, "Let it go, buddy. Drop it in." And the kid drops the ball through the hoop. The kid's like, "I did it! I slammed the basketball through the hoop!" As adults, we know what really happened. The two-year-old kind of did it, but without his dad, the toddler couldn't do anything. The basketball is almost bigger than he is. He barely held on—he simply let go at the right time.

That's the way we are. When we do good things, we're like, "Wow, I'm so good. I helped that person. I prayed. I showed up to Mass. I did it." We did good things, but this is because God was working inside of us. That's the mystery. It's such a gift. Every time you and I do something good, it's because God's grace was already at work in us. Every time you and I show up to pray, it's because God invited us to prayer.

When we go to Mass or pray or go to confession, we are like that child whose father lifts him up to the basketball hoop. It is God who brings us there. God wants us there. If it wasn't for his grace, his complete gift, we wouldn't be there. But sometimes we get lifted up to the hoop and just hold on to the ball. Our Father is like, "Go ahead. I'm making all of this possible." His love has brought us there, and he continues to bring us there.

After the child puts the ball through the hoop, what does the dad do? He says, "Let's do it again." He gives the kid the ball again and lifts him up, and the kid gets to do it again and again. And the more he does that, the more the kid says, "Do it again," and the more the dad does it.

This is the mystery of going from lifelessness to being saved, from lifelessness to having that active participation in what God is doing on this earth. Imagine being able to look in the mirror and saying, "Lord, you've just got to keep lifting me up. You keep letting me dunk. I could not even dream of dunking, but you keep lifting me up." That's what he did to get you to read this booklet. That's what he does every time you say yes to him.

SHOW UP TO GIVE

God saves us from lifelessness. He saves us from quiet desperation. He takes us from collecting and prepares us to give. But I know sometimes people think, "Well, I don't have anything to give, so I'll wait until I have more. Then I'll offer something significant."

Dave Ramsey is a financial advisor with a radio show, and people call into his show and say things like, "You know, Dave, I'm worried about getting rich because I always associate rich people with being jerks." Dave says, "Listen. I know a lot of poor people. I know a lot of rich people. Money just makes you more of what you already were before you had money. So if you're a grumpy, stingy poor person, you're going to be a grumpy, stingy rich person. If you're a jerk as a poor person, you'll be a bigger jerk as a rich person because you have more money to be a jerk with. But if you're a generous poor person, you're going to be a generous rich person."

This is true when it comes to the spiritual life, too. If I'm not willing to give when I have a hundred dollars, I'm not going to be willing to give when I have a hundred thousand dollars because I'm holding on. If I'm just here to get that hundred, then I don't have anything to spare when I have a hundred thousand. If I'm not willing to give when I have a little, I'm not going to be willing to give when I have a lot.

It's easy to say, "I'm too poor; I don't have anything to give." My invitation this week is to look at all the places that you and I typically show up to "get" and say, "OK, God, where can I give? What can I offer here?"

Usually I go to work or to class to get something—instead, I'm going to show up and say, "What can I offer? What can I give here?" When I spend time with my friends, I usually show up because I really like spending time with them. My attitude is, "What can I get here?" Instead, I'm going to show up and say, "What can I give here?"

Realize the power of looking like the Son. The Son came to give his life as a ransom. Imagine this week being saved from lifelessness because you and I decided to show up and to ask,

"Where can I give?" That is another way to say, "How, in this situation, can I look like Jesus?"

REFLECT

Have you ever collected anything? If you haven't, what is something you might like to collect? Why?

Can you think of a recent experience where you decided not to do something because you didn't think you were going to get anything out of it (going to class, going to Mass, getting together with family, prayer, etc.)? Did you regret not doing it?

Have you ever had a discussion with a non-Catholic about the question of "faith and works" and the differences between Catholics and many Protestants with regard to salvation? How did it go? If you were to have a discussion now, what would you emphasize or say?

Thinking about the basketball analogy, where does grace fit into your life? Do you try to do it all on your own, or do you let God help you? Are you letting his gift of grace pick you up and give you life? Are you letting go of the ball instead of keeping the gifts you've been given for yourself? Are you asking him to pick you up and to help you again?

Even in our most broken moments *and deepest sufferings, through grace we still have something to give. Have you ever thought about how your sufferings can be an opportunity for self-giving rather than self-serving? What strikes you most about that?*

Have you ever *fallen into thinking that you'll give when you have more, but not right now? What's wrong with this way of thinking? How can we switch our mentality?*

ACT

Write down *a list of the places you usually go to receive something. Then, ask God what you can offer in those places and write down the answers.*

Chapter 5

SAVED FROM LOVELESSNESS

Who is one person you know loves you? I immediately think of my mom. Honestly, I've just been blessed by a lot of people who have cared for me and loved me—and my mom is at the top of the list. She's incredible.

When you know someone loves you, the next question is, "How do you know?" One way I know my mom loves me is what she did for me when I was growing up. Every day, she would go into the kitchen where there was a fireplace and make a fire before my siblings and I got out of bed. Then she would make us breakfast every single morning and supper every single night. And if we were home from school, she'd make lunch. I knew my mom loved me because she did that even when she was sick. I thought this was normal. I remember the first time I ever went to school, I talked to some kids who were saying something about having Pop-Tarts that morning or making their own breakfasts. I was like, "What? You made your own breakfast? Doesn't your mom love you?" It just shocked me.

A couple of years ago, my older sisters told me something about my mom: she hates cooking. I never knew this. Not only did my mom make meals even though she detests cooking, but she didn't show that she hated it. When I found that out, I was like, "Wow, she really loves me because she did something for me without complaining, without even giving me the slightest indication that she didn't like it."

My mom did this for my siblings and me consistently. Her actions told me that she loved me.

LOVE LANGUAGE

The way we know people love us is through their actions or through their presence. We know it either because they're doing something or because they're showing up and just being there.

In fact, the only way that you and I have ever known love is through our bodies. Now, you might be like, "Duh, yeah," but this is important for us to understand. The only way you and I have ever known anything actually is through our bodies. You either saw something, heard something, tasted it, smelled it, or felt it. You got it into you through your body.

An author named Gary Chapman wrote a book called *The Five Love Languages*. Basically, he popularized the theory that people have various ways to communicate love to other people and receive love. He describes five of them. One is quality time—just spending time and being present. Another one is gift-giving. Some people are really touched in their hearts by gifts, and that's how they express love. A third is acts of service. A fourth love language is words of affirmation. Some people just love to hear how much you love them. A fifth one is physical affection.

We all have these different ways of communicating and receiving love. But every single one of them happens to us through the body. Each is communicated to us and proven to us by what someone did or by their very presence. So if someone asks you, "Are you loved?" you can point to something you experienced through your body and say, "That's how I know."

HOW DO YOU KNOW?

We've been talking about what Jesus saves us from. He saves us from sin and death. He saves us from fatherlessness, hopelessness, and lifelessness. Here, we're going to talk about this: Jesus saves us from lovelessness.

JESUS SAVES US FROM LOVELESSNESS.

When someone asks you if you are loved, a follow-up question is, "How do you know?" When someone asks you if you are saved, that has the same follow-up question. How do you know you're saved? Is it a matter of having a sense of general peace? Do you just feel saved?

You can answer that question by pointing to a specific moment two thousand years ago in Israel. You can say, "I know I'm saved because Jesus died on the Cross and because he rose from the dead." Pointing to that event in history is a great answer. Jesus is the source of our salvation. He is the source of every grace. That's what caused our salvation to be possible.

But have you ever wondered how the death and resurrection of Jesus—what he did two thousand years ago, halfway around the world—can have anything to do with you right now? Yes, he saved humanity two thousand years ago, half a world away. But how does that have anything to do with my life? How does it make any difference here and now? Do you ever wonder that? So do I.

THE SACRAMENTS

Here's the answer. Through the sacraments, the Holy Spirit makes actual what Jesus made possible. The sacraments that have been given to us make the past saving action of Jesus present in our lives right now.

THE SACRAMENTS MAKE THE SAVING ACTION OF JESUS PRESENT IN OUR LIVES RIGHT NOW.

In fact, I would say this: the sacraments are necessary for salvation. This might sound really bold, but it is the absolute truth. In order for what Jesus did two thousand years ago to make any difference in your life and in my life right now, the sacraments are necessary. We need them. The sacraments make present what Jesus had done in the past for every single one of us.

Think about how God saved the world. When you were a kid with your brothers and sisters or friends, did you ever call your chair "saved" when you got up to leave the room? Like, "That chair's saved! It's mine! You can't take it!" God can do anything. He could have just called the world saved. But that is not how God saved the world.

Instead, Jesus took on a body and lived in that body. He suffered in that body. He died and rose and ascended to heaven in that body, and we were saved through his body. Now, how do you experience that salvation? Through your body, not just in your mind. When was the last time you had a real transformational event that happened only in your mind? Never. The way to translate what Jesus did two thousand years ago to your life right now is through your body—through the sacraments.

BORN AGAIN

Someone can say, "Well, yeah, but Father, I believe, and I really feel it. Why do I need the sacraments?" Feeling close to God is really good. But think about this: Loving another person doesn't make you married to that person. Really, really loving that other person doesn't make you married. Really feeling like you're married doesn't make you married. What makes you married to that person is marrying that person. You have to actually go through the motion of the wedding.

In Second Timothy chapter 1, St. Paul writes to Timothy, "Rekindle the gift of God that is within you through the laying on of my hands" (2 Timothy 1:6). St. Paul is describing the day Timothy was ordained. He is saying, "Timothy, remember the day I made you into a priest of God? Fan into flame that gift that I gave you through the imposition of my hands, body to body." Timothy knew he was a priest because St. Paul laid his hands on him in the sacrament of Holy Orders.

June 6, 2003, is the day I was made a priest. It's not because I really felt it that day or because my schooling was done that day. What happened was the bishop called me forward, and I received the sacrament of Holy Orders through the laying on of the bishop's hands. I can point to that specific day and say, "That was the day I was made a priest."

So when were you saved? I was saved on March 1, 1975, in Bloomington, Minnesota. That's the day I was baptized. At that moment, what happened two thousand years ago happened to me. What Jesus made possible two thousand years ago was actually made present in me. I can point to that specific moment because the sacraments are necessary for salvation.

The day you were baptized is the day you were saved.

> ## THE DAY YOU WERE BAPTIZED IS THE DAY YOU WERE SAVED.

This isn't just me saying this. This is what Jesus tells us in the Gospel of John. Jesus says, "Unless one is born of water and the Spirit, he cannot enter the kingdom of God" (John 3:5). Unless you're baptized, you can't enter the kingdom of heaven.

> ## "UNLESS ONE IS BORN OF WATER AND THE SPIRIT, HE CANNOT ENTER THE KINGDOM OF GOD"
> (John 3:5).

In the Acts of the Apostles chapter two, Peter goes out and preaches on Pentecost day to three thousand people. They're cut to the heart, so they ask, "What must we do to be saved?" Does Peter say, "Just have a warm feeling"? No, St. Peter says, "Repent and be baptized for the forgiveness of your sins" (Acts 2:38). What must we do to be saved? Repent and be baptized.

In fact St. Peter writes in his first letter that Baptism "now saves you" (1 Peter 3:21). So when were you saved? At your baptism. How do you know you were saved? Not because you feel it but because you were baptized. The Holy Spirit working through the sacraments makes the Son's past actions present. What he made possible, the sacraments make actual.

TRANSFORMED

At this point, you might be wondering about something. If you remember, I talked about how I didn't like church until I had a conversion experience at age fifteen or sixteen. You could say, "Father, it sounded earlier like you said you were saved when you were fifteen or sixteen years old." But no. I had an awareness of the baptism that I was brought into; it became alive in that moment, and I received God's grace in the sacrament of Reconciliation—but it all goes back to my baptism. It all goes back to March 1, 1975.

It all comes from the fact that when you and I were baptized, we were actually transformed. St. Peter says that when you're baptized, you become a partaker in the divine nature (see 2 Peter 1:4). St. Paul says you become a new creation (see 2 Corinthians 5:17). You might say you're not just Homo sapiens, you're Homo sapiens plus Baptism. You're a whole different thing because now your soul has been divinized. You've been transformed.

WHEN YOU AND I WERE BAPTIZED, WE WERE ACTUALLY TRANSFORMED.

Baptism transforms you because the sacraments aren't merely ceremonies. They're God's actions in this world.

MANNA

If you say, "I don't know if I'm loved," just look to the sacraments. How do you know you're loved? Because the sacraments are God's actions, and they are God's presence to you.

And yet so often we couldn't care less. It's frustrating to have to recognize that so often we're just like the Israelites. Do you remember the story of how the Israelites were set free from slavery in Egypt? They're led through the Red Sea into the wilderness where they're so hungry, they think they're going to die. And God takes care of their needs. He brings them bread from heaven every single day for forty years. The Israelites walk out of their tents every morning and see this food on the ground that they call manna. But after a while—not even a long time—the Israelites start to complain. They're like, "Why do we have to eat this bread from heaven?"

Think about how irrational that is. First of all, this manna is keeping them alive. It is the only thing between them and death by starvation, yet they're complaining about it. Second, it's a free gift from God. He doesn't have to give them this. Third, the manna is proof that God loves them. Every morning the Israelites walk out of their tents and see on the ground this sign of his love. Every morning, they can see that God is faithful. He has not abandoned them. He's present and acting.

And yet the Israelites couldn't care less. They see this gift as a burden. I used to read that story and think, "That's crazy. Who would ever think that?" But then I realized: that's me. God keeps proving his love again and again, and I see this gift—this proof of his love—as an imposition and a burden.

Jesus is the new bread from heaven. In the Gospel of John, Jesus says, "It was not Moses who gave you the bread from heaven; my Father gives you the true bread from heaven" (John 6:32). The people listening to Jesus say, "OK, great. Send us this true bread from heaven." Then he tells them, "I am the living bread which came down from heaven; if any one eats of this bread, he will live for ever; and the bread which I shall give for the life of the world is my flesh" (John 6:51). The new bread from heaven is the Eucharist that we can receive at every Mass.

Then Jesus goes on. He says, "Unless you eat the flesh of the Son of Man and drink his blood, you have no life in you" (John 6:53). Remember: the sacraments are necessary for salvation. The sacraments are the way that God communicates his salvation to us. That is why Jesus says this. No one goes into heaven without this gift from God.

This gift is God's very life that gives us eternal life. But how do we respond? Often we think, "Why do I have to go to Mass again on Sunday? I don't have time for this." It has become a burden for many of us. We see it as an imposition.

That's one of the things that deeply grieves me: how indifferent we can be to the life of grace. We can be indifferent to this offer of salvation in the sacraments. In so many ways, this is basically indifference to love. So many of us are wandering through the world asking, "Doesn't anyone love me?" And God is trying to get our attention, saying, "Absolutely, I do. Here is proof."

SAVED FROM LOVELESSNESS

I think many of us are so hungry that we've forgotten that there is actually food for us. We're so parched and thirsty that we've forgotten that God has actually given us something to drink. We are so wounded and broken that we can't see that God wants to save and heal and forgive us in confession.

So we put up walls. When I say, "The sacraments are necessary for our salvation," I know that some of us become defensive and say, "Wait, what about people who didn't get baptized? What about someone who's not Catholic and can't receive Holy Communion or doesn't go to confession?" Somebody can even object, saying, "Father, you know, I read in the Bible that Jesus told the good thief he was going to be with him in paradise. He wasn't baptized on the cross, so why are you saying baptism is necessary?" In our woundedness, we try to put those walls up so that we don't have to face the fact that the sacraments are necessary for us.

Here's what the Church teaches about this. The *Catechism* says, *"God has bound salvation to the sacrament of Baptism, but he himself is not bound by his sacraments"* (CCC 1257, original emphasis). The Church teaches that God has bound himself to his sacraments. This means that every time his sacraments happen, he has promised that he will be there. But he is not bound by a sacrament, so can he save anyone, even if that person is not baptized or doesn't go to confession? Yes, he can do that; he's God.

But then I hear people say, "Oh, then I'll take that option. That's the extraordinary way, and I want the extraordinary way." Why do we tend to say this? Why do we put up walls and turn away from the sacraments? Because this gift of love has been wasted on us. We see it as a burden.

The reality is this: we can meditate on Jesus' life and his redemption by reading the Bible and praying, and we can hope and trust in him. That's really good. Do that. Please do that. But we can also encounter the very saving action of Jesus in the sacraments, where he saves us from a life of lovelessness.

God wants you to know that you're loved. He wants you to know it, and he wants you to live it. He doesn't want you to go through another day doubting the fact that he loves you.

THE SACRAMENTS ARE NECESSARY FOR SALVATION. WE CAN ENCOUNTER THE VERY SAVING ACTION OF JESUS IN THE SACRAMENTS, WHERE HE SAVES US FROM A LIFE OF LOVELESSNESS. GOD WANTS YOU TO KNOW THAT YOU'RE LOVED, AND HE WANTS YOU TO LIVE IT.

WHAT DO YOU WANT?

I was talking to a man once who was raised Catholic but left the Faith. He was away for a long time, but he came back home to the Catholic Church. He went to confession, and it was a big moment. Afterward, he told me, "Father, for all those years when I was away from the Catholic Church, I knew I had sin, and I wanted to be forgiven. So I would go into my room and play songs that made me feel sad for my sins until I felt like I was sad enough. Then I'd switch to songs that promised God's mercy and hope and healing. I'd play those songs and pray until I felt like I was forgiven. So first I made myself feel sad and then I made myself feel forgiven. When I went to confession after all that time, honestly, Father, I didn't really feel anything—but I know I'm forgiven. I know it because I can point to that sacrament and say, 'Jesus was there. He saved me again.'"

God wants you to live in contact with his love on a daily basis. He wants to save you from fatherlessness, from hopelessness, from lifelessness, and from lovelessness. So he gives you and me the sacraments as the proof that he loves us. They are his actions in the world. They are his presence in the world.

He wants to save you. The question is this: do you want to be saved? He wants to love you in the sacraments. Do you want him to love you?

GOD WANTS TO SAVE YOU.
THE ONLY QUESTION IS THIS:
DO YOU WANT TO BE SAVED?

REFLECT

Who is one person you know loves you? How do you know that person loves you?

The five love languages—how someone prefers to receive love—are words of affirmation, quality time, physical touch, gifts, and acts of service. What are your primary love languages?

Through the Holy Spirit, Jesus conveys his own love language: the sacraments. What does that mean to you? How does God love us through the sacraments?

To be indifferent to the sacraments is to be indifferent to love. Is the spirit of indifference something that you wrestle with? How can someone work through that indifference?

Have you had a powerful experience when you encountered God's love in one of the sacraments? How did it strengthen your relationship with God?

Have you ever put walls up between yourself and the sacraments? If so, why do you think that is?

Now how would you respond if someone asked you, "Are you saved?"

What are your biggest takeaways about the salvation Christ has won for you?

ACT

Find a local church or adoration chapel and make a holy hour. Reflect on these closing questions: "Do you want to be saved? Do you want God to love you?" Jesus has saved you from sin, fatherlessness, hopelessness, lifelessness, and lovelessness. Ask him to help you live in a way that reflects the freedom he has won for you!

REMEMBER

- Jesus is the Savior. We are all broken by sin, so Jesus came to save us from our sins. Salvation means that he saves us from being un-Christ-like.

- Jesus saves us from fatherlessness because Baptism brings us into the relationship that the Son has with the Father. God makes us his beloved sons and daughters. We are adopted children of God.

- Because of our sins, we all owe a debt that we cannot pay, so Jesus paid a debt he did not owe. He saves us from the hopelessness that comes along with indebtedness. We are redeemed.

- Jesus saves us from lifelessness and wants us to be agents of his mercy. We are saved by grace through faith working in love.

- In the sacraments, Jesus saves us from lovelessness. We are transformed and saved in Baptism. The sacraments are necessary for salvation.

NOTES

1   See Michael Patrick Barber, *Salvation: What Every Catholic Should Know* (Greenwood Village, CO: Augustine Institute, 2019).

2   See US Treasury, "Debt to the Penny," available at fiscaldata.treasury.gov.

3   See Melanie Hanson, "Student Loan Debt Statistics," July 10, 2021, available at educationdata.org.

4   See Bill Fay, "Demographics of Debt," May 6, 2021, available at debt.org.

5   St. Cyril of Alexandria, *On the Unity of Christ* (Crestwood, NY: St. Vladimir's Seminary Press, 1995), 59.

6   See kolbeshrine.org and saintmaximiliankolbe.com.

7   Henry David Thoreau, *Walden; or, Life in the Woods* (Boston: Ticknor and Fields, 1854).

8   John Paul II, *Salvifici doloris* (February 11, 1984), 27.

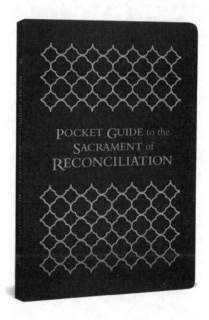